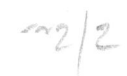

R. VAUGHAN WILLIAMS

'A ROAD ALL PAVED WITH STARS'

ADAPTED AND ARRANGED BY
ADRIAN WILLIAMS

STUDY SCORE

MUSIC DEPARTMENT
OXFORD
UNIVERSITY PRESS

OXFORD
UNIVERSITY PRESS

Great Clarendon Street, Oxford OX2 6DP,
United Kingdom

Oxford University Press is a department of the University of Oxford.
It furthers the University's objective of excellence in research, scholarship,
and education by publishing worldwide. Oxford is a registered trade mark of
Oxford University Press in the UK and in certain other countries

The Poisoned Kiss © Oxford University Press 1936, 1957
This orchestral arrangement © Oxford University Press 2016

Publication kindly supported by The Vaughan Williams Charitable Trust

The Moral Rights of the Composer and of the Arranger of this Work have been asserted
in accordance with the Copyright, Designs and Patents Act, 1988

First published 2016

Impression: 1

All rights reserved. No part of this publication may be reproduced,
stored in a retrieval system, or transmitted, in any form or by any means,
without the prior permission in writing of Oxford University Press

Permission to perform this work in public
(except in the course of divine worship) should normally be obtained from
a local performing right licensing organization, unless the owner or the occupier
of the premises being used already holds a licence from such an organization.
Likewise, permission to make and exploit a recording of these works
should be obtained from a local mechanical copyright licensing organization

Enquiries concerning reproduction outside the scope of the above
should be directed to the Music Rights Department, Oxford University Press,
at music.permissions.uk@oup.com or at the address above

ISBN 978-0-19-340985-9 (study score)
ISBN 978-0-19-340142-6 (on hire)

Printed in Great Britain

PREFACE

A Road All Paved with Stars is an orchestral synthesis of the music from Vaughan Williams's opera *The Poisoned Kiss* (1936), the title coming from one of the central arias, in which Amaryllus sings of his love for his sweetheart Tormentilla. The score was jointly commissioned by The Vaughan Williams Charitable Trust and Oxford University Press.

My brief was for a work which would easily fit into the average concert programme, so that the best music from the opera might be introduced to a wider public. The music for the most part sits in 'light opera' territory, although the central second act owes more to grand opera, and contains supremely wonderful music. I knew immediately that I wanted to keep more or less intact the sections leading up to the 'fatal' Kiss, the Kiss itself, and its aftermath—these form the opera's core. Vaughan Williams himself had composed an overture which contains 'orchestra-only' takes on many of the most memorable songs and sections, and I was tempted to use some of these—but he didn't include any of the most glorious Act 2 music. Only once I had decided to begin my piece with that Act 2 material, growing gloriously, sunrise-like out of darkness, did the first third or so of *A Road All Paved with Stars* begin to take shape. Part of the brief was to stick as far as possible to the opera's story line: I largely achieved this, whilst using certain melodic figures such as 'Tormentilla' as leitmotifs. All the while I was aware that I needed to build towards the Kiss climax, and the whole of that central sequence is included.

I was left with the question of how to 'descend' satisfactorily from the passion of the Kiss and the death music, creating a final section which did not seem short-changed. Without a 'happily-ever-after' ending the work could have concluded at that point, which would have meant omitting all the glorious music from Act 3 (including the great finale which Vaughan Williams had included in his overture)—but my piece really needed a happy ending! My solution was to move directly from the death music to the finale of Act 3, in an instant jolting the listener out of the sombre mood. The finale music became a framework within which to capture some of Act 3's great moments, notably the Empress's aria 'Love breaks all rules'. Noting this was in E flat, I could not resist the shift into a restatement of 'Blue larkspur in a garden', in A flat, from Act 1, just before the concluding return of the finale music.

Adrian Williams

ORCHESTRATION

2 Flutes (second doubling Piccolo)
2 Oboes
2 Clarinets (in B♭)
2 Bassoons
4 Horns (in F)
2 Trumpets (in C)
3 Trombones
Tuba
Timpani (3 drums)
Percussion (3 players: Xylpohone, Glockenspiel, Side Drum,
    Cymbals, Suspended Cymbal, Tambourine, Bass Drum, Tam-Tam,
    Triangle, Frusta)
Harp
Strings

TRANSPOSING SCORE

Duration: *c.*27 minutes

In memory of Michael Kennedy (1926–2014), friend of Vaughan Williams and champion of his music.
A Road all Paved with Stars was jointly commissioned by Oxford University Press and The Vaughan Williams Charitable Trust.

'A ROAD ALL PAVED WITH STARS'

A SYMPHONIC FANTASY
based on music from the opera *The Poisoned Kiss* by Ralph Vaughan Williams

original music by R. VAUGHAN WILLIAMS
adapted and arranged by ADRIAN WILLIAMS

The Poisoned Kiss © Oxford University Press 1936, 1957. This orchestral arrangement © Oxford University Press 2016.

10

18

24

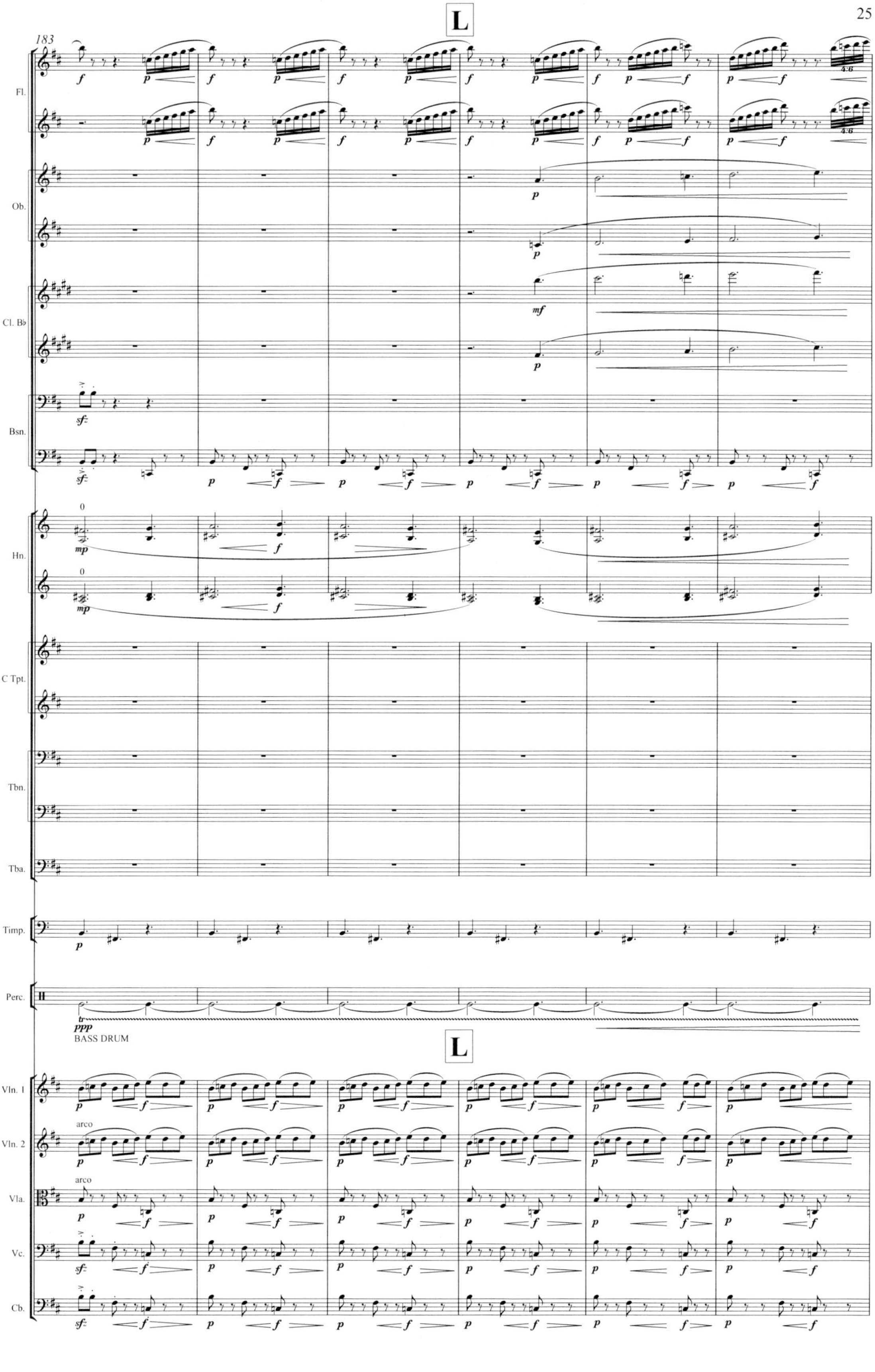
L
183
Fl.
Ob.
Cl. B♭
Bsn.
Hn.
C Tpt.
Tbn.
Tba.
Timp.
Perc.
BASS DRUM
L
Vln. 1
Vln. 2
arco
Vla.
arco
Vc.
Cb.

più mosso ♩ = 142
230
Fl.
Ob.
Cl. B♭
Bsn.
Hn.
a 2
C Tpt.
a 2
Tbn.
Tba.
Timp.
tr
Perc.
D major
Hp.
più mosso ♩ = 142
Vln. 1
Vln. 2
Vla.
Vc.
Cb.

O
ancora più mosso ♩ = 156
238
Fl.
Ob.
Cl. B♭
Bsn.
Hn.
C Tpt.
Tbn.
Tba.
Timp.
Perc.
Hp.
marc.
(a 2)
a 2
S.D.
pizz.
arco
Vln. 1
Vln. 2
Vla.
Vc.
Cb.

allargando 𝅗𝅥 = 56
P
245
Fl.
to PICCOLO
Ob.
Cl. B♭
Bsn.
Hn.
a 2
C Tpt.
Tbn.
Tba.
Timp.
Perc.
GLOCKENSPIEL
Hp.
allargando 𝅗𝅥 = 56
P
Vln. 1
Vln. 2
Vla.
Vc.
Cb.

36

37

Q
278
Fl.
Picc.
Ob.
Cl. B♭
Bsn.
Hn.
C Tpt.
Tbn.
Tba.
Timp.
Perc.
Hp.
Vln. 1
Vln. 2
Vla.
Vc.
Cb.
Solo
espr.
TRI.
pizz.
arco
Q

292
Fl.
Picc.
Ob.
Cl. B♭
Bsn.
Hn.
C Tpt.
Tbn.
Tba.
Timp.
Perc.
Hp.
Vln. 1
Vln. 2
Vla.
Vc.
Cb.
Solo
a 2
S.D.
arco
pizz.
cresc.
dim.

40

Andante con moto ♩. = 72
317
Fl.
ppp
Ob.
p cant.
Cl. B♭
ppp
pp
Bsn.
p espr.
Hn.
ppp
pp
C Tpt.
con sord.
p
Tbn.
Tba.
Timp.
Perc.
Hp.
C♮, D♮, E♭, F♭, G♭, A♭, B♮
pp
Andante con moto ♩. = 72
senza sord.
Solo
arco
Vln. I
arco
div a 3
con sord. (solo senza sord.)
ppp
gli altri div.
arco
Vln. 2
unis.
div.
con sord. unis.
Solo
senza sord.
mf espr.
Vla.
(unis.)
gli altri
arco con sord.
arco con sord.
pizz.
Vc.
Cb.

42

327
S
Fl.
Ob.
pp
Cl. B♭
pp
Bsn.
pp
Hn.
1
C Tpt.
mp
Hp.
S
Solo
mf
4
Vln. I
senza sord.
Vln. 2
senza sord. poco a poco
tutti
Vla.
p
Vc.
f
pizz.
f
Cb.

44

45

347
T
Fl.
Picc.
Ob.
Cl. B♭
Bsn.
Hn.
C Tpt.
Tbn.
Tba.
Timp.
Perc.
Hp.
Vln. 1
Vln. 2
Vla.
Vc.
Cb.
TAMBOURINE
B♭
E♭
nat.
A♯, B♮♭C♯, D♯, E♮
arco
(pizz.)
arco

355

U
poco rit.
Allegretto ♩= 118
363
Fl.
Picc.
to FLUTE
Solo
Cl. B♭
Bsn.
Hn.
(4)
C Tpt.
stacc. sim.
Tbn.
Tba.
con sord.
Timp.
Susp. CYM.
Perc.
XYLO.
rubber sticks
Hp.
G major
G♮
U
poco rit.
Allegretto ♩= 118
Vln. 1
sul pont.
nat.
div.
Vln. 2
Vla.
(div.)
IV
Vc.
pizz.
arco Solo
Gli altri div.
arco
unis.
Cb.
arco
div.
1 desk

372
V
Fl.
Cl. B♭
Solo
p
Bsn.
Solo
pp espr.
p
Hn.
C Tpt.
Tbn.
Tba.
Timp.
Perc.
Hp.
V
Vln. 1
unis.
pp
Vln. 2
unis.
pp
div.
unis.
Vla.
unis.
pp
div.
mf
unis.
pp
Vc.
(Solo)
p
p espr.
(gli altri)
pp
Cb.
Tutti div.
pp
unis., pizz.

385
Fl.
Ob.
Cl. B♭
Bsn.
(1)
Hn.
1
Tbn.
Hp.
Vln. 1
Vln. 2
div.
unis.
Vla.
Vc.
(Solo)
(gli altri)
Cb.
arco
pizz.
pp
p
mf
mp

W
398
Fl.
FLUTE
to PICCOLO
Ob.
Cl. B♭
Bsn.
Hn.
Tbn.
senza sord.
cantabile
Hp.
G♯
W
Vln. 1
div.
unis.
Vln. 2
div.
Vla.
unis.
Vc.
(Solo)
cant.
(gli altri)
Cb.
arco
pizz.
arco

X
412
Fl.
Picc.
PICCOLO
to FLUTE
Ob.
Cl. B♭
Bsn.
Hn.
C Tpt.
Solo
senza sord.
Tbn.
Timp.
Hp.
G major
sub. pp
Vln. 1
Vln. 2
Vla.
Vc.
Cb.
div.
(Solo)

427
Y
Andante con moto,
poco più mosso (in 3)
Fl.
FLUTE
pp
Ob.
Cl. B♭
Bsn.
Hn.
p
C Tpt.
(con sord.)
senza sord.
Tbn.
dolce
Timp.
Hp.
Vln. 1
div.
ppp
Solo
p dolce
gli altri
Vln. 2
con sord.
div.
con sord.
Vla.
Solo
con sord.
gli altri
con sord.
Vc.
con sord.
Solo
p dolce
Cb.

440
Z
Fl.
Ob.
Cl. B♭
Bsn.
Hn.
Timp.
Perc.
Hp.
C, D♭, E♭, F♭, G♭, A♭, B♭
ppp
p cant.
(Solo)
(Gli altri)
Vln. 1
Vln. 2
Vla.
Tutti, div.
senza sord.
mp cant.
Vc.
con sord.
senza sord.
Cb.

55

AA
451
Fl.
cresc.
tr
Ob.
Cl. B♭
Bsn.
Hn.
C Tpt.
Tbn.
Tba.
senza sord.
(Tri.)
Susp.CYM.
GLOCK.
Perc.
Hp.
E♮, G♮
AA
(Solo)
(Gli altri)
Vln. 1
Vln. 2
(div.)
Vla.
(senza sord.)
Vc.
arco
Cb.

Maestoso ♩ = 76
455
Fl.
Ob.
Cl. B♭
Bsn.
Hn.
a 2
C Tpt.
Tbn.
Tba.
Timp.
Perc.
GLOCK.
Hp.
C major
Maestoso ♩ = 76
unis.
Vln. 1
Vln. 2
Vla.
Vc.
Cb.
cresc.

BB
463
Fl.
Ob.
Cl. B♭
Bsn.
Hn.
C Tpt.
Tbn.
Tba.
Timp.
Perc.
Susp. CYM.
Hp.
poco arpegg.
F♯, C♯
BB
Vln. 1
Vln. 2
div.
Vla.
Vc.
Cb.
pizz.
arco

473

483
Fl.
to PICCOLO
Ob.
Cl. B♭
Bsn.
Hn.
C Tpt.
Tbn.
Tba.
Timp.
Perc.
Hp.
Vln. 1
unis.
Vln. 2
unis.
Vla.
div.
unis.
Vc.
Cb.
arco
pizz.
arco
pizz.

CC
molto rit. a tempo
492
Fl.
Picc.
Ob.
Cl. B♭
Bsn.
Hn.
C Tpt.
Tbn.
Tba.
Timp.
Perc.
Hp.
Vln. 1
Vln. 2
Vla.
Vc.
Cb.
PICCOLO
to FLUTE
a 2
CYMBALS
gliss.
+8ves
cresc.
div.
unis.
arco

DD
Allegro vivace ♩. = 144
502
Fl.
Ob.
Cl. B♭
Bsn.
Hn.
a 2
C Tpt.
con sord.
Tbn.
Tba.
Timp.
(tr)
Perc.
Susp. CYM.
S.D.
Hp.
Vln. I
Vln. 2
Vla.
Vc.
Cb.
sul pont.
sul pont., div.
nat.
unis. nat.
cresc.
sub. f
fpp
fp
pp
mf

63

Adagio ♩ = 78
EE
516
Fl.
Ob.
Solo
Cl. B♭
Bsn.
Hn.
a2
C Tpt.
Tbn.
Tba.
Timp.
Perc.
TAM-TAM
damp
Hp.
Adagio ♩ = 78
EE
Vln. 1
Vln. 2
Vla.
pizz.
arco
Vc.
div.
unis., pizz.
arco
Cb.
pizz.
arco

65

526

66

GG
Allegro moderato
♩ = 100
545
Fl.
to PICCOLO
Ob.
p espressivo
Cl. B♭
Bsn.
Hn.
C Tpt.
f
senza sord.
f
Tbn.
con sord.
p
(con sord.)
p
pp poco
Tba.
Timp.
tr
ppp molto
f
S.D
tr
ppp molto
tr
f
CYM.
Perc.
Hp.
E major
dolcissimo
p
pp
GG
Allegro moderato
♩ = 100
Vln. 1
(unis.)
Solo
pp dolcissimo
Gli altri
pp
div.
ppp
ppp
Vln. 2
pp
ppp
Vla.
div.
p
pp
ppp
Vc.
pizz.
div.
arco
p
pp
arco
ppp
Cb.
pp
ppp

68

569
Fl.
Picc.
Ob.
Cl. B♭
Bsn.
Hn.
C Tpt.
Tbn.
Tba.
Timp.
Perc.
Hp.
G major
Vln. 1
Vln. 2
Vla.
Vc.
Cb.
IV
ord.

II
577
Fl.
Picc.
Ob.
Cl. B♭
Bsn.
Hn.
C Tpt.
Tbn.
Tba.
Timp.
Perc.
Hp.
Vln. 1
Vln. 2
Vla.
Vc.
Cb.
to FLUTE
TRI.
B♭
poco meno mosso
div.
unis.
Solo
Gli altri
div.
pizz.

71

poco più animato
597
Fl.
Ob.
Cl. B♭
Bsn.
Hn.
con sord.
C Tpt.
Tbn.
Tba.
Timp.
Perc.
Hp.
B♮
poco più animato
Vln. 1
Vln. 2
Vla.
Solo
Gli altri
appass.
Vc.
Cb.
arco
pizz.
div.
arco
(pizz.)
unis.
arco

73

LL
619
Fl.
Ob.
Cl. B♭
Bsn.
Hn.
C Tpt.
Tbn.
Tba.
Timp.
Perc.
Hp.
Vln. 1
Vln. 2
Vla.
Vc.
Cb.
cresc.
senza sord.
4 senza sord.
a 2
con sord.
F♯, A♯
A♮
B♭
(unis.)
arco
pizz.

75

MM
poco rit.
poco meno mosso ♩= 72
634
Fl.
to FLUTE
Ob.
Cl. B♭
p espr.
pp
Bsn.
pp
p
Hn.
C Tpt.
Tbn.
mf leggiero
pp
Tba.
Timp.
Perc.
Hp.
MM
poco rit.
poco meno mosso ♩= 72
Vln. 1
p molto espress.
pp
Vln. 2
mp
p molto espress.
pp
Vla.
p molto espress.
pp
Vc.
div.
unis.
p molto espress.
pp
Cb.
p molto espress.
pp

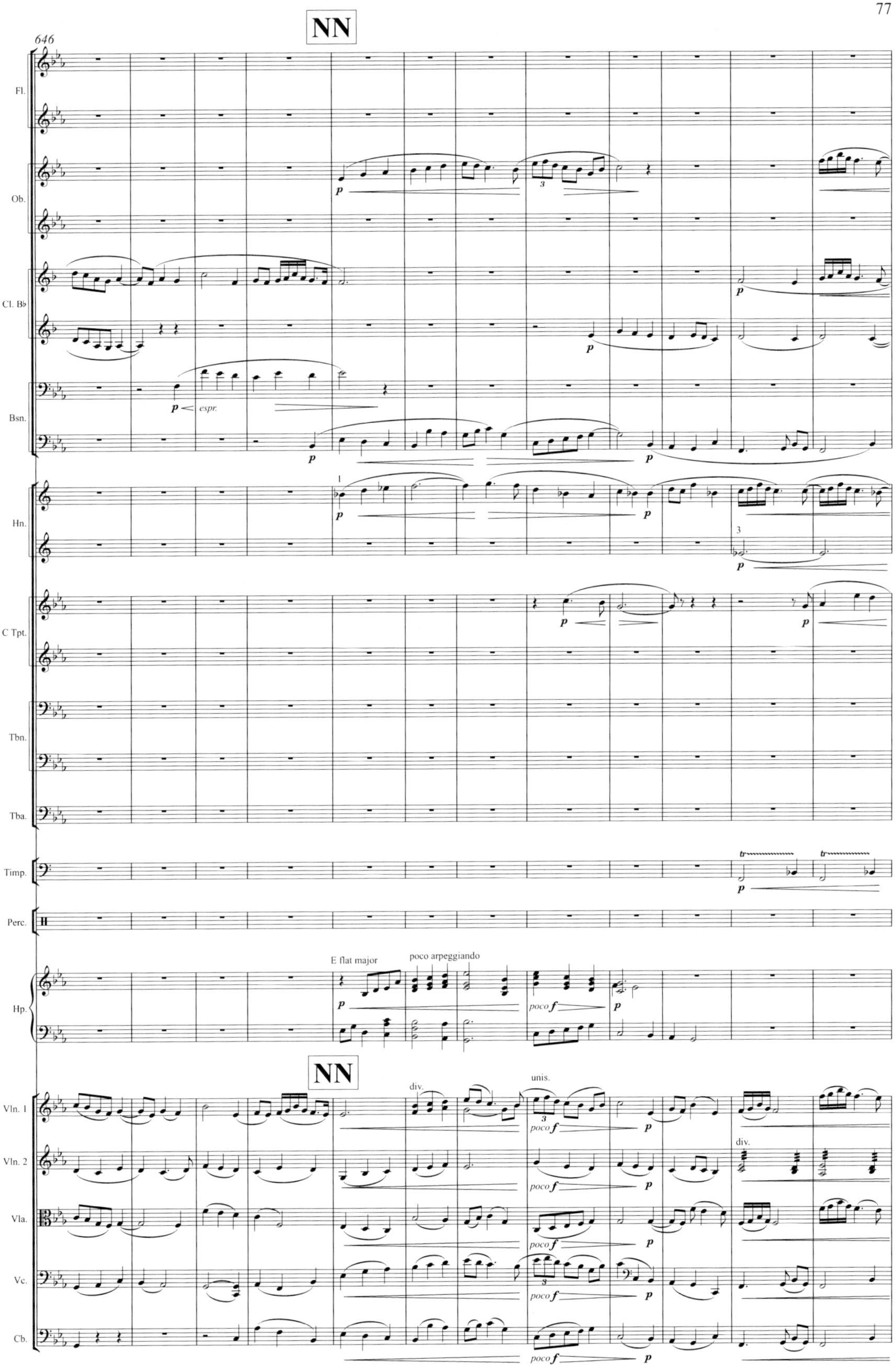

78

OO
poco stringendo
666
Fl.
Ob.
Cl. B♭
Bsn.
Hn.
C Tpt.
Tbn.
Tba.
Timp.
Perc.
Hp.
Vln. 1
Vln. 2
Vla.
Vc.
Cb.
mf marc.
p
a 2
p sost.
tr
poco
p cresc.
f
OO
poco stringendo

Allegro vivo ♩= 112
674
Fl.
to PICCOLO
PICCOLO
Ob.
Cl. B♭
Bsn.
Hn.
C Tpt.
con sord.
senza sord.
Tbn.
Tba.
Timp.
Perc.
Susp.CYM.
Hp.
A♮
B♮, F♯, C♯
leggiero
Allegro vivo ♩= 112
Vln. 1
Vln. 2
Vla.
Vc.
Cb.
div.
unis.
pizz.
arco

81

82

duration *c.*24 minutes